Baptism
with the
Holy Spirit

Biblical Truth Simply Explained

Baptism with the Holy Spirit
Jack Hayford

Biblical Meditation
Campbell McAlpine

Blessings and Curses
Derek Prince

Deliverance
Bishop Graham Dow

Forgiveness
John Arnott

The Holy Spirit
Bob Gordon

Prayer
Joyce Huggett

Rejection
Steve Hepden

Spiritual Protection
Lance Lambert

The Trinity
Jack Hayford

Trust
Tom Marshall

Worship
Jack Hayford

Baptism with the Holy Spirit

Jack Hayford

Chosen Books

A Division of Baker Book House Co
Grand Rapids, Michigan 49516

Copyright © 2001, 2003, 2004 Jack W. Hayford

Published in the USA in 2004 by Chosen Books
a division of Baker Book House Company
P.O. Box 6287, Grand Rapids, MI 49516-6287
www.bakerbooks.com

This text abridged from selected chapters of *Grounds for Living,* copyright
2001 Jack Hayford. Originally published by Sovereign World Limited of
Tonbridge, Kent, England.

Printed in the United States of America

Library of Congress Cataloging-in-Publication Data
Hayford, Jack W.
    [Grounds for living]
    Baptism with the Holy Spirit / Jack Hayford.
        p. cm. — (Biblical truth simply explained)
    Originally published: Grounds for living. Tonbridge, Kent, England:
Sovereign World, 2001.
    ISBN 0-8007-9348-X (pbk.)
    1. Baptism in the Holy Spirit. I. Title. II. Series.

BT123.H35 2004
234'.13—dc22

                                                        2003063494

Notes for Study Leaders

This book is intended to give a biblical background to the baptism with the Holy Spirit and also to help each reader personally experience this gift of God. Five study questions at the end of each chapter are designed to stimulate thought and challenge each person about their personal response to the Holy Spirit and His gifts. Praying together and asking for God's help will help everyone to grasp the truths presented.

Don't be surprised if different opinions and responses arise among your group during this study, particularly when answering certain questions. As a leader you will need to balance the needs of individuals with those of the whole group. It is wise not to get sidetracked into devoting too much time to any one person's thoughts but to enable everyone in the group to share and respond to the positive message of the book. If the study takes place in an encouraging and receptive atmosphere, it will help people feel more able to share openly.

Encourage group members to read one chapter prior to each meeting and think about the issues in advance. It is usually good to review the content of the particular chapter at the meeting, however, to refresh everyone's memory and to avoid embarrassing those who have not managed to do the reading in advance.

Our hope is that as readers think and pray through the subject of the baptism with the Holy Spirit, their personal understanding of God will increase and cause them to be more fruitful in all areas of their lives. May God bless you as you study this material yourself and lead others in doing so.

Contents

1

River of Release

What makes a believer, after they have come to Christ, continue to live like a believer? It is the fact that the truth is incarnate in them. The truth goes on living and growing inside them, and they begin to grow and change. This is the ministry of the Holy Spirit working in the life of the believer.

Although we all receive the Holy Spirit when we believe in Christ, Jesus spoke of a baptism with the Spirit that would overflow to everyone around us. This baptism is a river of release and blessing which we can all receive.

The Person and the Power

The Holy Spirit has been poured out upon the Church that we might receive power and enabling from on high, as Jesus promised. The first chapter of Acts reveals two vital reasons why Jesus gave the gift of the Holy Spirit to us. "You will receive power when the Holy Spirit comes on you; and you will be my witnesses in Jerusalem, and in all Judea and Samaria, and to the ends of the earth" (Acts 1:8).

He Makes His Life Manifest in Us
Jesus gave us the power of the Holy Spirit so that His life would become manifest in us. This life is evidence that Jesus

is not dead but alive and still ministering in the world today. The Holy Spirit verifies this as we give testimony to others of our experience of Christ and as Jesus is manifest in our lives through our character and actions.

He Continues His Ministry through Us

The Holy Spirit was also lavished upon us so that the ministry of Jesus would continue through us. Jesus seeks to work through each believer by the power of the Holy Spirit so that the Father's will is accomplished. As He continues His ministry on earth, we are His hands and feet.

Please note two important points here:

1. It is impossible for the *person* of Jesus to be manifest in our character except by allowing the Holy Spirit to come in and dwell with us.

2. We cannot have the *power* of Jesus flowing through our lives unless the Holy Spirit comes and overflows in us.

In other words, the Holy Spirit comes to indwell the believer so that the person of Jesus can be seen in us, and He overflows our lives so that the power of Jesus can move through us. All that Jesus came to do and say continues through us as we cooperate with the Holy Spirit.

Jesus' Dual Role as Savior-Messiah

Jesus had two distinct roles to fulfill as the prophesied Messiah: He came as the *Redeemer* and also as the *Restorer*.

The most fundamental human need relates to our lost condition without God, which was brought about by our sin. We need forgiveness, redemption, cleansing and a way back to God. Our sin destroyed the intimate relationship Adam and Eve enjoyed with God before the Fall. Therefore all human beings need a Redeemer to settle the debt of our sin and reinstate the purity of our relationship with God.

Our sin not only severed our relationship with God but also our position of rulership in life. Bereft of the power to live life the way it is supposed to be lived, human beings are in desperate need of a Restorer.

Jesus comes as the Lamb of God who takes away the sin of the world but also as the one who baptizes with the Holy Spirit. Hereby we meet the Savior, who will save us through His death on the cross, transferring His righteousness to us. But we also meet the Baptizer, who will restore us by transmitting His power for ministry through us.

Jesus comes to pour out the same Spirit upon us that anointed Him and made Him the Messiah and King, so that the power of that kingdom life will be upon us also and enable us to rule in life.

The baptism with the Holy Spirit, then, is an intrinsic part of the restoring aspect of Jesus' dual role. It is something that He desires to do in us after redemption has taken place. By it He equips us with all the fullness of His life. Jesus gives us *forgiveness* and then imparts *fullness*.

Overflowing with the Spirit will affect everything we do. Whatever God has put within us of the life of His Son may now begin to be powerfully lived out, as we touch the world with His love in real and tangible ways.

The Holy Spirit Dwells Within and Overflows in Believers

The Bible makes a clear distinction between the Holy Spirit *dwelling within* a believer and the Holy Spirit *baptizing* a believer and *overflowing in* a believer's life. We can verify this by examining two clear facets of the Holy Spirit's character and work.

The Spring of Water

The first feature of the Holy Spirit occurs *within* us to satisfy the thirst in our life. This happens as we are saved. In John 4:13–14, Jesus said to the Samaritan woman at the well, "Everyone who drinks this water will be thirsty again, but whoever drinks the water I give him will never thirst. Indeed, the water I give him will become in him a spring of water welling up to eternal life."

The Holy Spirit is described as indwelling us like an inner fountain or well at which we drink to find the answer for our own personal need. Notice that the word *spring* is singular—it refers to something for our personal need.

The Streams

The second feature of the Holy Spirit flows *outward* to serve the needs of others. The overflow of our lives makes us tributaries of Christ's life to satisfy other people's thirst.

In John 7:37–39, Jesus is recorded as saying:

> "If anyone is thirsty, let him come to me and drink. Whoever believes in me, as the Scripture has said, streams of living water will flow from within him." By this he meant the Spirit, whom those who believed in him were later to receive. Up to that time the Spirit had not been given, since Jesus had not yet been glorified.

The Holy Spirit is described here as empowering the believer to reach out, to serve, to witness, to love, to give. This is the flowing out of God's life into others.

Note that the word *streams* is plural, as we will be equipped to meet many needs of many people. This second aspect of the Holy Spirit's nature and work is not intended merely to satisfy our own thirst. It is intended to flow out of us like a river that will touch other people.

Study questions:

1. How does both the person and the power of Jesus come to us through the baptism with the Holy Spirit?
2. Why do we need a Restorer as well as a Redeemer?
3. In what way does the Holy Spirit dwell within us as a fountain or well?
4. In what way is the Holy Spirit like streams of water flowing from us for the benefit of others?
5. Have you experienced this river of release and blessing? Explain.

2

The Terminology

We use the phrase "the baptism with the Holy Spirit" to describe how the believer is filled and overflowed with the Holy Spirit. Before looking more at this topic, we will discuss the term itself.

It is important that we learn about the words used in the Bible to describe this fundamental aspect of our life in Christ. Sometimes we can become so familiar with biblical terms that we lose sight of the richness of their meaning. So where did the phrase "baptism with the Holy Spirit" come from?

John the Baptist Introduced It
John the Baptist's ministry was to herald the Messiah. He announced that the Messiah had come to save His people. In identifying Jesus, he made two observations.

In John 1:29 he declared the saving and redeeming work of the Messiah: "John saw Jesus coming toward him and said, 'Look, the Lamb of God, who takes away the sin of the world!' "

In John 1:32–34 he declared the empowering and enabling work of the Messiah:

I saw the Spirit come down from heaven as a dove and remain on him. I would not have known him, except that the one who sent me to baptize with water told me, "The man on whom you see the Spirit come down and remain is he who will baptize with the Holy Spirit." I have seen and I testify that this is the Son of God.

Jesus Used These Words

Jesus Himself asserted, "For John baptized with water, but in a few days you will be baptized with the Holy Spirit" (Acts 1:5).

The terminology is not as important as the experience. The Bible uses at least six other expressions to describe this same event throughout the remainder of the book of Acts. Therefore it would be a mistake to dogmatically insist that this phrase is the only one that properly describes the infilling of the Holy Spirit. However, it is significant that Jesus used the words "baptism with the Holy Spirit" as an overarching term that encompasses all of the other biblical descriptions of the same event.

Looking Toward the Day of Pentecost

We have already seen that Jesus told His disciples that they would be baptized with the Holy Spirit "in a few days." These words, recorded by Luke, point us toward a definition of the baptism with the Holy Spirit.

Luke was a very precise historian and did not use words recklessly. Later in Acts 1:15 he said, "In those days . . . " As a writer, he maintained the flow of his narrative by increasing the reader's anticipation of an event in the days immediately approaching. But before the Holy Spirit was to come, there was first a process of prayer and preparation.

In Acts 2, we read that "the" day had finally arrived. Luke began to describe the time to which Jesus had referred: "When the day of Pentecost came . . . " With hindsight, the historian knew that this day was pivotal, and because of his careful record we are not left to wonder what the baptism with the Holy Spirit is.

As the Holy Spirit came, one hundred and twenty of the first believers were "baptized with the Holy Spirit." This was exactly that which had been predicted long ago by the prophet Joel: "In the last days, God says, I will pour out my Spirit on all people" (Acts 2:17).

The Meaning of the Word *Baptized*

This "pouring out" or "overflowing" is one of the six terms used to describe the experience of baptism with the Spirit, just as Acts 2:4 describes that all the disciples were "filled with the Holy Spirit." An examination of the Greek word translated *baptism* gives us further insight into its meaning and the harmony between it and the other terms used.

The word *baptized,* from the Greek word *bapto,* means literally "to dip." It describes a process of complete submersion and is the same word used to describe a sunken ship. Not only is the boat in the water, but the water is in the boat! This is not a casual sprinkling.

Jesus comes to immerse us in the Holy Spirit. Through baptism with the Spirit we have been placed into the working realm of the Holy Spirit, but we have also been filled *with* the Holy Spirit as the image of the sunken ship implies. This filling comes about as the Holy Spirit is poured upon us until we are overflowing.

Such an overflow of the Spirit only comes to people who open themselves up to God and are willing to receive it.

People who are spiritually hungry and thirsty enough will experience the flow of God's Spirit. But it can't be received in fullness by having just a quick shower—we need to be willing to get in the river and stay there!

Six terms are used in Acts: *baptized, poured out, given, received, filled* and *come upon.* They all combine in the word *baptize.* As Jesus baptizes us, the Holy Spirit is "poured out" (lavishly available to all who come) and "given" (presented freely), to those who "receive" (openly yield themselves to) His "filling" (complete overflowing) as He "comes upon" (fully embraces) them.

Together, these six words richly fulfill Jesus' prophecy in John 7:37–39:

> On the last and greatest day of the Feast, Jesus stood and said in a loud voice, "If anyone is thirsty, let him come to me and drink. Whoever believes in me, as the Scripture has said, streams of living water will flow from within him." By this he meant the Spirit, whom those who believed in him were later to receive. Up to that time the Spirit had not been given, since Jesus had not yet been glorified.

As believers experience the inflow of "streams of living water," they will be released in an outflow of ministry to the world.

Baptism of or Baptism with?

Some people often use imprecise terminology for the baptism *with* the Holy Spirit, calling this experience the "baptism *of* the Holy Spirit." Although it may seem a trivial difference, it can cause confusion about who exactly does the baptizing. Let us try wherever possible to use clear expressions that accurately describe what the Bible teaches.

Using the phrase "baptism of the Holy Spirit" implies that it is the Holy Spirit who is doing the work of baptizing. However, John said that this is Jesus' work. It is Christ Jesus who gives us this baptism with the Holy Spirit.

When we realize that Jesus is the One who baptizes us with the Holy Spirit, we are able to have a richer understanding and deeper perspective on this experience. It shifts our recognition from the idea that it is "something that happens to me" to understanding that it is "Someone who ministers to me." That someone is Jesus Himself!

So we can see that this experience:

- Is not strange or impersonal. (It is a Person-to-person encounter with our loving Lord.)

- Is not to be feared. (Satan will use fear to keep us from anything good that God wants to do in our lives, anything that causes us to grow.)

- Is a distinct event. (We come to Jesus, trusting Him and simply asking Him to baptize us with the Holy Spirit.)

When we begin to think in these terms, we will no longer see being baptized with the Holy Spirit as an "experience" as such, but as just a natural part of coming to Jesus and receiving all of the fullness that He intends for our lives. We can lay aside all anxiety about when and how it might take place and just let Jesus be in control.

The Manifestations of Pentecost

Jesus told His disciples that the baptism He promised would take place in just a few days. When the day came and the power of the Lord fell upon them and filled them, a whole series of things began to happen in their lives.

- They "began to speak in other tongues as the Spirit enabled them" (Acts 2:4).

- A large crowd was attracted and became curious, asking what it was all about (Acts 2:12).

- Peter was gifted to preach the Scriptures with revelatory insight (Acts 2:14–40).

- Multitudes repented and accepted the message of Christ (Acts 2:37, 41).

- There was fervent devotion to the Word of God, to the sacraments, to prayer and to fellowship (Acts 2:42, 46).

- Miracles occurred and continued to take place in the lives of the believers. They moved in a spirit of faith that could only have been brought about by the Holy Spirit (Acts 2:43).

- The love of God was manifest in the community of believers as they began caring for each other sacrificially (Acts 2:44–45).

- A constant stream of people continued to come to the faith day by day (Acts 2:47).

These are just a few of the new beginnings for those who were baptized with the Holy Spirit. And Jesus wants His Church to experience such things today, just as in the book of Acts.

Study questions:

1. How is the phrase "baptism with the Holy Spirit" an overarching phrase that encompasses other terms for the same experience?

2. What does the Greek word *bapto* tell us about the experience of baptism?

3. Why is it significant that we are baptized *with* the Holy Spirit?

4. What manifestations followed the outpouring of the Spirit at Pentecost?

5. Are you experiencing these same things in your own Christian life?

3

The Timing

Having discussed the terminology of the baptism with the Holy Spirit, let us now discuss its timing.

The Breath of God

The baptism with the Holy Spirit is a distinct experience in the life of a believer in Jesus Christ. John 20:22 is a critical verse in understanding this. It says: "And with that he [Jesus] breathed on them and said, 'Receive the Holy Spirit.'" Jesus spoke these words to His disciples late in the first night that He appeared to them after the resurrection.

The disciples were secretly gathered together, fearing what might happen to them now that Jesus was gone. To their surprise, Jesus appeared to them and commissioned them to carry out His work on the earth. As He called them to receive the Holy Spirit, His words were joined with an action—He breathed on them. This was a highly significant act.

When God created Adam, the Bible tells us that "the LORD God formed the man from the dust of the ground and breathed into his nostrils the breath of life, and the man became a living being" (Genesis 2:7).

God breathed His life into human beings. When they sinned and died spiritually, the breath of God (the Holy

Spirit) departed from them and all that remained was the physical breath of their nostrils.

Isaiah alluded to this in a passage in which he warned against dependency on human resources. This is the way the prophet poetically expressed it: "Stop trusting in man, who has but a breath in his nostrils. Of what account is he?" (Isaiah 2:22).

Jesus' resurrection from the dead signified that now redemption had been completely accomplished. The transition from the old covenant to the new had been made. Just as the old creative order began with the breath of God, so now the new creative order that Jesus was establishing began with divine breath. As 1 Corinthians 15:22 says, "For as in Adam all die, so in Christ all will be made alive."

So we see that on this night, as soon as the full provision of redemption was completed, Jesus visited His small band of believers and breathed the life of the new creation into them—the Holy Spirit. Some interpret these actions as merely symbolic, alluding to the Day of Pentecost still to come, but the Greek words denote the immediacy of the action. Jesus was saying, "Receive the Holy Spirit *right now.*"

Even though Jesus breathed the Holy Spirit into the disciples then, He still told them to wait in Jerusalem before beginning their mission, because the baptism with the Holy Spirit would happen to them later. It was a distinct and future experience. He said, "I am going to send you what my Father has promised; but stay in the city until you have been clothed with power from on high" (Luke 24:49).

Timing

The experience of being filled or overflowed with the Holy Spirit applies to all believers. However, in the breadth of

Christian tradition, different doctrinal views have been expressed about the way this baptism relates to conversion. There are three main views:

1. That the baptism with the Holy Spirit is an event that happens simultaneously with salvation.

2. That salvation and the baptism with the Holy Spirit are two separate and distinct events (although they may occur at the same time).

3. That the baptism with the Holy Spirit happened one time only on the Day of Pentecost in order to bring to birth the early Church.

If the baptism with the Holy Spirit automatically occurred at the point of salvation, then John the Baptist would not have separated the dual aspects of Jesus' ministry. In fact, as we have already seen, he heralded "the Lamb of God who takes away the sin of the world"—who brings salvation—and announced that "this is he who baptizes with the Holy Spirit"—the one who empowers His followers.

This is the first of many verses of Scripture that point to a separate and distinct event. It does not mean that the two events may not be very closely fused in an individual's experience. With some, receiving Christ as Savior and being baptized with the Holy Spirit happens at virtually the same time. For many others, there is a period of time between the two events, perhaps coinciding with the time of answering Jesus' call to be baptized in water.

A Neglected Experience

Many people today have received Jesus Christ as their Savior and yet have not been baptized with the Holy Spirit. This also happened in the early Church, as we see in Acts 8:4–17. It gave concern to the leaders of the first churches, and it should concern us now.

Philip had been preaching Christ to the people of the city of Samaria, and many believed, including a leader of occult activity, Simon the sorcerer. Although these people had been baptized in water, they did not receive the "outpouring" of the Holy Spirit right away. Acts 8:14–17 tells us:

> When the apostles in Jerusalem heard that Samaria had accepted the word of God, they sent Peter and John to them. When they arrived, they prayed for them that they might receive the Holy Spirit, because the Holy Spirit had not yet come upon any of them; they had simply been baptized into the name of the Lord Jesus. Then Peter and John placed their hands on them, and they received the Holy Spirit.

Whenever a person receives Jesus Christ as Savior, the Holy Spirit has already done a tremendous work in them. First Corinthians 12:3 tells us, "no one can say, 'Jesus is Lord,' except by the Holy Spirit." The new believers were baptized and by implication made a genuine confession to the Lordship of Christ in their lives.

These crowds were unquestionably saved and had received the Holy Spirit to dwell in them. What had not yet happened to those Samaritans, however, was the overflowing of the Holy Spirit in all His fullness.

Similarly, when the apostle Paul came across a group of believers in Ephesus, he asked them, "Did you receive the Holy Spirit when you believed?" (Acts 19:2). This was because he detected that something was missing from their lives. In fact, they had not even heard of the Holy Spirit! Paul promptly taught them right doctrine, baptized them into the name of the Lord Jesus, and "when Paul placed his hands on them, the Holy Spirit came on them, and they spoke in tongues and prophesied" (Acts 19:6).

We know that Luke, the writer of the book of Acts, was with Paul in his travels and would have been present when this happened. He carefully recorded the event, along with the similar event in Acts 8. This makes it clear that the apostles were concerned not only that believers would come to know the certainty of Christ *in* their lives, but also the multiplying ministry of Christ *through* their lives.

In a very real sense, when we ask for the baptism with the Holy Spirit, we say to God, "I not only want the person of Jesus made real in my life by Your Holy Spirit, but I also want the power of Jesus to work through me." We should be as eager for this as the leaders of the early Church were. The good news is that Jesus is the Baptizer with the Holy Spirit, and He says that He wants this to happen to every one of His own.

Study questions:

1. Why is God's breath significant in terms of creation and the fall of humanity?
2. When Jesus breathed on the disciples, how did it complete the redemption that He had come to bring?
3. How do we know that conversion and baptism with the Holy Spirit are distinct events, even if they may be closely linked in time?
4. What was Paul's response to believers who had not yet received the Holy Spirit?
5. Have you received the baptism with the Holy Spirit? If so, when did it happen?

4

The Terms of Receiving

As I began to speak, the Holy Spirit came on them as he had come on us at the beginning.

Acts 11:15

We continue our study of the baptism with the Holy Spirit by examining the terms—the basic requirements of heart-preparedness before Jesus pours out His Holy Spirit on a person.

Of course, the Lord is ready to baptize with the Spirit all who come to Him in faith. His terms are rooted in grace and abundantly attainable. They do not have to do with achievement, but attitude. They represent a stance of the heart rather than status.

Available to All

The whole tenth chapter of Acts is the background for our study because it illustrates so wonderfully how God is willing to pour out His Holy Spirit on all those who meet His terms. It tells the story of Cornelius, a centurion of a regiment of the Roman army. He and all his household are described as "devout and God-fearing" (Acts 10:2).

Cornelius received a vision in which an angel of God told him to send for the apostle Peter. The next day, even as members of Cornelius's household were on their way to find Peter, Peter himself was given a vision from God. It was about midday and shortly before the main meal of the day, so Peter was hungry. In the vision, the Lord offered Peter animals to kill for food, but Peter refused because those animals were considered "unclean"—forbidden for the Jews to eat. Nevertheless, the Lord said three times, "Do not call anything impure that God has made clean" (Acts 10:15). Still puzzling over the meaning of the vision, Peter was persuaded by the Holy Spirit to go with Cornelius's servants.

Cornelius was a Gentile who was hungry to know God and look more deeply into spiritual matters. Although he was serving as a Roman soldier, a foreigner, in that area of Judea he was exposed to the Jews whom God had raised up as His own people.

It appears that Cornelius was not ignorant of the fundamentals that had to do with Jesus (verses 36–38). He had heard the Good News preached, but he had never had the truth confirmed to him. Peter assured Cornelius that what he had heard about Jesus was indeed true and made the message of salvation very clear. Cornelius responded positively, because while Peter was still speaking, an astounding thing happened! The Holy Spirit was spontaneously poured out on those Gentiles.

As Acts 11 opens, we find Peter returning to Jerusalem to explain to a bewildered church what had happened. For the first time, Gentiles (who did not observe rituals of the Old Testament law) had received the same work of the Holy Spirit that the disciples had received at Pentecost. Reporting back, Peter said:

"As I began to speak, the Holy Spirit came on them as he had come on us at the beginning. Then I remembered what the Lord had said: 'John baptized with water, but you will be baptized with the Holy Spirit.' So if God gave them the same gift as he gave us, who believed in the Lord Jesus Christ, who was I to think that I could oppose God?"

When they heard this, they had no further objections and praised God, saying, "So then, God has granted even the Gentiles repentance unto life."

Acts 11:15–18

So for the first time, Gentiles opened their hearts to the testimony of the Savior-Messiah, and suddenly the Holy Spirit came upon them. This momentous event marked a major transition in the life of the Church as it began to grasp the idea of a global vision. First, God had broken down walls in Peter's heart by the vision he had received (Acts 10:9–16), and subsequently He had broken down walls in the hearts of the other Jewish believers.

Until that time, the body of the early Church was entirely populated by Jewish believers. This was the first real impact that was made upon the Gentile community, and it was a stunning upheaval for the leaders of the church in Jerusalem. Of course it was also a significant breakthrough in the fulfillment of the words of Jesus—that His Gospel would be taken to all the world as a witness to the nations.

Some years later, this led to the convening of the Council in Jerusalem to settle once and for all the issue of the observance of Mosaic Law in the Church (Acts 15:6–29). Before that day in Caesarea, they more than likely assumed that Jesus' commission was limited to the Diaspora (those Jews scattered around the world), not Gentile people of the nations of the world.

The disciples now began to understand more of the full

implications of Jesus' words when He said, "You will receive power when the Holy Spirit comes on you; and you will be my witnesses in Jerusalem, and in all Judea and Samaria, and to the ends of the earth" (Acts 1:8).

Terms of Receiving

The story of Cornelius and his household reveals the terms, or qualities of soul, that are important for a person to receive the fullness of the baptism with the Holy Spirit. Yet we must bear in mind that everything we receive from God comes by grace. This grace flows upon those who come before the Lord with an attitude of utter dependency.

We can draw four qualities from this passage.

Obedience: Wanting God's Will

Cornelius was a devout man who feared God. We must notice the difference between a person who is trying to earn something *from* God, and one who simply has a heart *for* God. *Devout* means "wholehearted." Cornelius had a simple, genuine reverence for God—a fear or healthy respect for Him.

Cornelius did not yet have a full relationship with God, as we would think of it. However, although he had not yet been born again, his heart was open to God, and he desired to be obedient. He cared generously for the poor, and he prayed regularly.

While we must guard against the universalist idea that all mankind is seeking the same God by different pathways, we must surely avoid the small-minded attitude of supposing that God pays no attention to the heart-cries of those who don't yet know Jesus. God is merciful and responsive to the needs of His creatures, and He is willing to show Himself to them. The apostle Paul spoke of such God-fearing people in Romans 2:14—people who have little or no knowledge of God's law, but who live by principles that reflect His law.

The Bible says there is only one way to God—through Jesus Christ. Salvation does not encompass many different routes to God. Cornelius needed to have the gaps in his theology filled in by Peter, so that he understood exactly what Jesus did for him and how he must come to Him in obedience.

Humility: Wanting God's Way

As Cornelius received Peter into his home, he gathered the members of his household together and said to Peter, "I sent for you immediately, and it was good of you to come. Now we are all here in the presence of God to listen to everything the Lord has commanded you to tell us" (Acts 10:33).

This statement is full of childlike faith! Despite the fact that being a centurion, he could have asserted his status as a representative of imperial Rome, he acted in a most humble manner, and he was grateful and deferential to Peter for his kindness in coming. Further, Cornelius was effectively saying, "We are at your disposal to hear what God will say through you." In his humility he was honestly inquiring and simply wanted God's way.

People who desire the baptism with the Holy Spirit should come with an honest, humble heart, open before the Lord, trusting His servants and desiring all that He has for them.

Purity: Wanting God's Nature

In Leviticus 11:45, the Lord says, "I am the LORD who brought you up out of Egypt to be your God; therefore be holy, because I am holy."

At that stage, the people of God had been out of bondage

for only a matter of months. This was likely to have been written in the forty-day period during which Moses was up on Mount Sinai in God's presence receiving revelation from the Lord.

One of the most notable aspects of Leviticus is the repetition of God's words, "I am the LORD," a statement which occurs many times throughout the book. Why did God keep reminding His people of this fact? Because they needed to learn that He was different from all the other gods that pervaded the Egyptian culture in which they had been raised. They had now been delivered and were called to live a life apart.

God was saying, "I am different. My nature is different; My character is different. I am the Lord." He was emphasizing His holiness, and in so doing, His completeness and distinctness from all the false gods of the world. He calls us also to a heart attitude that will make us distinct from those living under the world's system.

Cornelius's lifestyle testified that he had a heart attitude of desiring God and His holiness (Acts 10:2). He aimed to be like God in character. Similarly, anyone who approaches the Lord wanting to be baptized in the Holy Spirit should be saying, "Lord, I want to be immersed in Your nature—the *Holy* Spirit." We have already seen that the word translated *baptism* means "to be completely immersed." God desires that we come to a place of being completely immersed in His holiness, and that we remain there, under the overflowing river of His Spirit.

The Holy Spirit comes to give us the power and authority of the living God. He also comes to bring purity and the refinement of Jesus' life and love. John the Baptist said of Jesus, "He will baptize you with the Holy Spirit and with fire" (Matthew 3:11).

Malachi, prophesying of the time when God would "suddenly" come to His holy temple, said, "He will be like a refiner's fire . . . as a refiner and purifier of silver" (Malachi 3:2–3).

On the Day of Pentecost, the disciples did actually have flames that looked like fire over their heads, symbolizing the purifying work of the Holy Spirit (Acts 2:3). God was suddenly occupying His temple—the Body of Christ, His Church. So on the day the Church was born, this temple was filled with the fire of God. The disciples received both *power* and *purity*, which was expressed in a *passion* to live in a way that reflected God's nature.

Beware of paying too much attention to teachers who emphasize the power and authority that believers possess, to the neglect of the purity to which we are called. It is true that we have power and authority, but unless these things flow through people who have been purged by the fire of God and exhibit righteousness and humility, it will be out of balance.

Authority and humility are mutually dependent, and without them both we can be either powerless or harsh and loveless. And we must not fall into the trap of questioning the purity of others, rather than examining ourselves, remembering that Acts 10:15 says, "Do not call anything impure that God has made clean."

The baptism with the Holy Spirit comes to those who want God's nature and are open to the cleansing work of the Lord in their lives, but this does not mean they must have attained perfection in purity. God declares that we are justified by faith in Him, and only through Christ are we declared holy. On these grounds alone a person is worthy to receive the fullness of the Holy Spirit. When we minister to a person who wants the baptism with the Holy Spirit,

the only requirement is that they have received Jesus as
Savior.

Receptiveness: Wanting God's Fullness

The final qualifier for receiving the baptism with the Holy
Spirit has to do with a willingness to receive. The word
receive occurs in Acts 10:47 as Peter described what had
happened to Cornelius and his household.

One of the most interesting aspects of the events that
took place in Cornelius's house is that they were baptized
with the Holy Spirit before they were baptized in water.
Why was this the case, given that we have already identified
water baptism as a key sign of obedience leading to receiving the fullness of the Spirit?

I believe that God in His grace decided to do things in that
order because Peter was still unsure whether these Gentiles
could really be saved without keeping the ordinances of the
Jewish law. The Lord poured out the Holy Spirit on them
prior to their water baptism as evidence of His grace being
lavished on all mankind. This was not the usual order of
things, and it is the only example of this sequence in the
entire Bible. And even here, believers were immediately
baptized in water.

It may be that people today have also been baptized with
the Holy Spirit before they have been baptized in water. This
is quite possible—who are we to put limitations on the way
in which God can work? However, even if this is so, it does
not take away the need to be baptized in water. Water
baptism is the command of Jesus.

For a person to receive the Holy Spirit presupposes an
attitude of openness and welcome to what God seeks to do
in him or her. Jesus described the essence of such an
attitude when He said, "Blessed are those who hunger and

thirst for righteousness, for they will be filled" (Matthew 5:6).

So these are the terms by which a person can receive the fullness of the Holy Spirit: obedience, humility, purity and receptiveness: wanting God's will, wanting God's way, wanting God's nature and wanting God's fullness.

Study questions:

1. In what way are God's terms for receiving the Holy Spirit "rooted in grace"?
2. What does the story of Cornelius tell us about the universality of this gift?
3. How does seeking God's will and way prepare us for the baptism with the Holy Spirit?
4. Why are purity and the Holy Spirit connected?
5. Do you have a heart attitude of openness and receptiveness toward the Lord?

5

The Tongues

While Peter was still speaking these words, the Holy Spirit
came on all who heard the message. The circumcised believers
who had come with Peter were astonished that the gift of the
Holy Spirit had been poured out even on the Gentiles. For they
heard them speaking in tongues and praising God.

Acts 10:44–46

Our discussion of the subject of speaking in tongues begins
where the earlier chapter left off, in the last few verses of
Acts 10. The power of God had spontaneously fallen upon
Cornelius and the members of his household, and they were
baptized with the Holy Spirit.

The Jewish believers who accompanied Peter to the
house of Cornelius were amazed. Not only was God pouring out His Spirit on these Gentiles, but specific things were
happening to them as they were filled with the Spirit:
"For they heard them speaking in tongues and praising
God."

Peter responded immediately by saying, "they have
received the Holy Spirit just as we have" (Acts 10:47).

God Chose This Gift for His Church

Jesus said:

> And these signs will accompany those who believe: In my
> name they will drive out demons; they will speak in new
> tongues; they will pick up snakes with their hands; and
> when they drink deadly poison, it will not hurt them at all;
> they will place their hands on sick people, and they will get
> well.
>
> Mark 16:17–18

Jesus' list of supernatural signs that testified to His presence
in a believer included speaking with other tongues. It is
important to note that Jesus Himself first introduced the
concept of speaking in tongues, considerably before the Day
of Pentecost. Also, on the Day of Pentecost, every single
disciple spoke in tongues, which gives us another insight
into its importance.

Although there are people who wish to minimize any
emphasis on this gift, we must recognize its value in God's
divine order. Speaking with tongues was the *birthmark* of
the early Church, and it is the *birthright* of every believer.
It is beyond our domain to preempt God's right to have
anything He wants in the life of the Church His Son died to
redeem. The gift of tongues is as much part of the plan of
God as it ever has been.

Paul makes this clear in 1 Corinthians 12:28:

> And in the church God has appointed first of all apostles,
> second prophets, third teachers, then workers of miracles, also
> those having gifts of healing, those able to help others, those
> with gifts of administration, and those speaking in different
> kinds of tongues.

A Gift for Our Good

Paul also emphasized its usefulness for the body of Christ, according to God's sovereign plan:

> Now to each one the manifestation of the Spirit is given for the common good. To one there is given through the Spirit the message of wisdom, to another the message of knowledge by means of the same Spirit, to another faith by the same Spirit, to another gifts of healing by that one Spirit, to another miraculous powers, to another prophecy, to another distinguishing between spirits, to another speaking in different kinds of tongues, and to still another the interpretation of tongues. All these are the work of one and the same Spirit, and he gives them to each one, just as he determines.
>
> 1 Corinthians 12:7–11

Paul also said, "I would like every one of you to speak in tongues..." (1 Corinthians 14:5). He was not saying this to make anyone feel guilty who did not speak in tongues, but he did commend those who did. Tongues were not intended as a proof of baptism with the Holy Spirit but as a resource for praise, prayer, worship and spiritual warfare (intercession).

Paul makes it clear that this gift is one that builds up the believer: "He who speaks in a tongue edifies himself" (1 Corinthians 14:4). A message in other languages can even build up the Church as a whole if it is interpreted when spoken aloud in a public gathering (1 Corinthians 14:5).

And note that the master-theologian Paul, the great spiritual intellect of the New Testament, gladly proclaimed that he spoke in tongues: "I thank God that I speak in tongues more than all of you" (1 Corinthians 14:18). Rather than apologizing for this edifying gift, he was very grateful for it and insisted that no one forbid believers to speak in tongues (1 Corinthians 14:39).

Jude adds an encouragement: "But you, dear friends, build yourselves up in your most holy faith and pray in the Holy Spirit" (Jude 20).

How Tongues Relates to the Baptism with the Holy Spirit

Fewer and fewer sectors of the Church debate any longer about whether God still performs miracles today, but there are still those who question whether believers should speak in tongues. However, I believe that evenhanded teaching of God's Word and sensitive ministry almost always lead people to an encounter with Jesus, the Baptizer with the Holy Spirit. In our experience the blessing of a spiritual language—speaking with tongues—attends virtually all who receive the fullness of the Spirit.

Throughout the Bible, the gift of speaking with tongues was so common as people were baptized with the Holy Spirit that there is no way you can honestly dissociate the two events. The important thing is that speaking with tongues is valid, valuable and vital where rightly discerned in truth, welcomed in experience and applied to life.

Although tongues are not a *qualification* for being acknowledged as "Spirit-filled," they are certainly an *indication* that the baptism with the Holy Spirit has taken place. Remember how in Acts 10, the Jewish believers were astonished because the Gentiles had spoken in tongues. It was a powerful indicator for them because they knew that they too had spoken in tongues the moment that they were baptized with the Holy Spirit.

We cannot disprove the classic Pentecostal doctrine that

the gift of tongues is the "initial physical evidence" that baptism with the Holy Spirit has taken place in a person's life, but we cannot conclusively prove it either. If a fellow Christian says they have been baptized with the Holy Spirit but are not yet speaking in tongues, we can expect that the same humility that brought them to that fullness will eventually cause them to be open to the further resources of the Spirit's gifts.

However, in ministering to people to receive the Spirit, we should engender faith for the full dimension of this experience. The entry of the beneficial, miraculous worship-praise-and-prayer language as enabled by the Spirit is fully biblical. Just as when Paul placed his hands on the believers at Ephesus, "the Holy Spirit came on them, and they spoke in tongues and prophesied" (Acts 19:6), we should expect spiritual gifts to follow the baptism with the Spirit.

Characteristics of the Spiritual Language

Looking at two qualities of the spiritual language of tongues will help us gain a better understanding of this precious gift of God. They are:

Majesty

There is a majesty to the spiritual language. Acts 10:46 says, "They heard them speaking in tongues and praising God." Acts 2:11 says, "we hear them declaring the wonders of God in our own tongues!" In both of these cases, people were praising and worshiping God and speaking of His greatness. It is the first biblical clue to the use of the gift of speaking in tongues.

There is nothing unworthy or common about this spiritual language. If speaking in tongues does no more than

enhance your personal expression of praise and worship to
God, then receive it gladly on that basis.

Miracle

It is a miracle that a person filled with the Holy Spirit should
have the ability to speak in another language, or even a
heavenly language. I believe that one of the key reasons why
God chose to manifest the gift of tongues at Pentecost was
that He wanted to literally put a miracle on their tongues—
something that transcended their natural abilities and
flowed from the fountainhead of God. They spoke with
other tongues supernaturally, "as the Spirit enabled them"
(Acts 2:4).

Speaking in tongues is a case of cooperation between
humanity and deity. We speak in a spiritual language
because we choose to allow the Holy Spirit to express
Himself through us in that way. He is the source, but we
choose to come to Him. God gives the gift, but we choose to
exercise it. God doesn't do anything in the Church without
our involvement and partnership with Him. "And pray in
the Spirit on all occasions with all kinds of prayers and
requests" (Ephesians 6:18).

In conclusion, there is a solid body of truth in Scripture
that supports the liberation of the believer into the use of
spiritual languages. At the birth of the Church the gift
of tongues was on the believers' lips, and still today the gift
is widely used as a resource for personal edification, praise,
worship and intercession.

Study questions:

1. When the Jewish believers heard Cornelius and his household speaking in tongues, what did it mean to them?

2. In what way is speaking in spiritual languages the birth-mark of the early Church and the birthright of every believer?

3. How is the gift of speaking in tongues valuable for the Church?

4. If tongues are not a qualification but an indication of the baptism with the Holy Spirit, how can we encourage receptiveness toward them?

5. Do you yourself have this miracle gift on your tongue? If so, do you use it and how does it benefit you?

6

Taking Hold of God's Gift

We can study and talk about the baptism with the Holy Spirit, but the most important thing is to receive it! This chapter will help every believer to take hold of this precious gift.

How Do People Receive the Holy Spirit?

The evidence of Scripture, and current practice in the Church today, suggests that the normal way in which a person receives the baptism with the Holy Spirit is through the ministry of another person praying and laying hands on them.

Peter and John laid hands on the Samaritan believers so they would receive the baptism with the Holy Spirit. Paul laid hands on a small group of believers in Ephesus and prayed for them to receive the baptism (Acts 19:6). People who are receptive to God are usually willing to receive prayer and ministry, and in this way millions of people around the world have received the baptism with the Holy Spirit.

However, the laying on of hands is not a legal requirement demanded by God. The book of Acts speaks of two incidents when no human contact was involved. No one laid hands on the disciples when they were first filled with the Holy Spirit, because there was no one to minister to them (Acts 2:4). Neither did Peter, having some trepidation about the situation in which he found himself, lay hands on the household of Cornelius.

These baptisms with the Spirit both happened spontaneously. While neither of these events could be described as being "normal"—the former signifying the birth of the Church, and the latter signifying the outpouring of God's grace upon the Gentiles—nevertheless there are many people who receive the fullness of the Holy Spirit without anyone praying for them. The laying on of hands is not compulsory.

Simon the Sorcerer

Acts 8 reminds us that purity of motive is important when we seek the fullness of the Spirit. Simon the sorcerer provides a case study of someone who had been saved and baptized in water, but who still displayed impure motives regarding the power of the Holy Spirit. He arrogantly thought he could buy the gift of God as if it was a commodity. He was still in bondage to the darkness of the occult—a "spirit of control" that characterized his past life. Peter rebuked Simon, saying:

> May your money perish with you, because you thought you could buy the gift of God with money! You have no part or share in this ministry, because your heart is not right before God. Repent of this wickedness and pray to the Lord. Perhaps he will forgive you for having such a thought in your heart. For I see that you are full of bitterness and captive to sin.
>
> Acts 8:20–23

Thankfully, Simon did repent, and answered, "Pray to the
Lord for me so that nothing you have said may happen to
me" (Acts 8:24).

What Is the Evidence?

How do you know when you have been filled and baptized
with the power of the Holy Spirit? The traditional Pentecostal test would be whether you had spoken in tongues.
However, the resource of speaking with tongues is not to
prove something has happened, but it is to praise and pray
with, to worship and wage warfare with.

The "sign" of tongues (Mark 16:15–17) is a precious gift.
Let us not get bogged down in doctrinal debate but be open to
the dynamic resources that this spiritual language provides.

Nevertheless, to those who are still earnestly asking,
"How will I know I have been baptized with the Holy Spirit?
What should I be looking for?" don't hesitate to look for the
benefit of tongues. They are biblical, they are practical and
they are beneficial. Expect this gift that was so freely poured
out from the hand of God from the very day the Church was
born.

Furthermore, expect something so clear in your experience of the power of God coming to you and overflowing
your life that you will know it. This is not just a matter of
having a "good feeling" or an "inner warmth." You may
have such physical feelings or you may not, but you will
know in your spirit that something has happened.

Finally, there may be other miraculous signs present. The
Holy Spirit comes to release the miracle life of Jesus through
us. You may experience the presence of other gifts of the
Spirit, such as prophecy. Or you may be suddenly set free
from something that has bound you for a long time and

which previously you were powerless to change. You may experience healing or freedom from a character trait such as anger or fear.

Receiving Now

If you, dear reader, have not already received the fullness of the Holy Spirit, let me urge you to come to Jesus now. Bow before Him, our precious Savior, and invite Him to baptize you with the Holy Spirit.

You can pray in your own words, or you may prefer this prayer as a guideline:

> Dear Lord Jesus,
> I thank You and praise You for Your great love and faithfulness to me. My heart is filled with joy whenever I think of the great gift of salvation You have so freely given to me. I humbly glorify You, Lord Jesus, because You have forgiven me all my sins and brought me to the Father.
> Now I come in obedience to Your call. I want to receive the fullness of the Holy Spirit. I do not come because I am worthy in myself, but because You have invited me to come. Because You have washed me from my sins, I thank You that the vessel of my life is worthy to be filled with the Holy Spirit of God.
> I want to overflow with Your life, Your love and Your power, Lord Jesus. I want to show forth Your grace, Your words, Your goodness and Your gifts to everyone I can.
> And so with simple, childlike faith, I ask You, Lord, fill me with the Holy Spirit. I open all of myself to You, to receive all of Yourself in me. I love You, Lord, and I lift my voice in praise to You. I welcome Your might and Your miracles to be manifested in me, for Your glory and unto Your praise. Amen.

"We are witnesses of these things, and so is the Holy Spirit, whom God has given to those who obey him" (Acts 5:32).

O Holy Spirit, come upon me,
Let Your grace and Your glory flow around.
As I bow at Jesus' feet now,
May the fire of heaven flood this holy ground.
As I worship here in full surrender,
Fill my life and my lips with highest praise.
Come fill me now!
Come fill me now!
O Holy Spirit, come upon me,
'Til my Jesus—my Lord and Savior, Jesus—
Fills all my ways with His praise,
All my days.

Jack Hayford

Study questions:

1. Is the laying on of hands necessary for receiving the Holy Spirit? Is it helpful?
2. What does the story of Simon the sorcerer tell us about right motives?
3. Which things can we look for as signs that the baptism with the Holy Spirit has taken place?
4. Have you prayed for and received the baptism with the Holy Spirit?
5. Are you able to lead others into this experience as well?

7

Ministering to Others

Have you ever wondered why Jesus never baptized anyone in water? He let His disciples do all the baptizing. I personally think it was because He did not want water baptism to be confused with the baptism that was His own—the baptism with the Holy Spirit. In Acts 1:4–5, Jesus distinguishes this baptism from the baptism of John: "Wait for the gift my Father promised, which you have heard me speak about. For John baptized with water, but in a few days you will be baptized with the Holy Spirit."

We have already seen how vigilant the leaders of the early Church were to see that new believers received this gift. The book of Acts shows that they immediately put it right if this reception had not occurred. The danger of discussing the baptism with the Holy Spirit is that we can keep it all at the level of theory. As believers we don't only want to be filled ourselves with the Spirit—we want to be sensitively available to minister to others who also want to be filled.

To give, we first need the resources. This includes a deep conviction about the importance and value of the baptism with the Spirit. It also involves an attitude of availability, so that when you find people who are open and hungry, you are ready to move in boldly. You can minister in confidence that the Lord will work *through* you, as He has worked *in* you.

We expect new believers to grow, just as we expect a baby to grow. If our children never moved on from helpless infancy, we'd be concerned. The baptism with the Holy Spirit releases a resource for growth and development in the Christian life.

Priests and Prophets

The Word of God tells us that we are called to be prophets— to speak the Word of the Lord. On the Day of Pentecost, Peter quoted the words of the prophet Joel: "Your sons and daughters will prophesy" (Acts 2:17). In prayer circles, on the job and in all sorts of other situations, the Holy Spirit gives you the things to say. He is calling you to minister the Word with life. The Word lives in you and comes forth with power.

We also read in the Scriptures that believers are a "chosen people, a royal priesthood, a holy nation, a people belonging to God, that you may declare the praises of him who called you out of darkness into his wonderful light" (1 Peter 2:9). Each one of us has a high commission from heaven, and it involves declaring our Lord's goodness to those around us.

Revelation 1:5–6 tells us that the same Lord Jesus who loves us and freed us from our sins by His blood "has made us to be a kingdom and priests to serve his God and Father." We are kings and priests, prophets and praying people. It is clear that God has given us the office of priest, but until we have the anointing, we are not installed in it.

Every one of us has an arena of government—we are in charge of something, including our own time and work.

Even if all you are responsible for is yourself, you still need the anointing of a king to exercise responsibility. But in fact virtually every one of us has some authority and responsibility over others in our families, employment, social circles, volunteer work and church life. Many people come under the power of who you are in the Kingdom of God, whether you realize it or not. The umbrella of your influence over other people means much. You must not try to dominate anyone else's will, but you can determine the kind of spiritual climate into which they come.

Some well-meaning discipling programs bring people under the domination of elders or pastors. Leaders are called to minister and admonish their flock in the faith and to manage people wisely, but not to control them. Where the Spirit is, there can be wise government that does not extinguish people's personalities. We are not to turn people into robots. Instead we are expressing the joy being poured out.

Steps in Ministry

Be Sure the Person Is Saved

This is not as obvious as you might think! In gatherings, people may respond to any call because they want something from God—they are hungry. They do not necessarily distinguish between one invitation and another. In my experience, at least one in ten who responds doesn't even know what they've come for. Ask them gently, "When did you ask the Lord Jesus to come into your life?"

Of course, some will say, "I've always believed." The Holy Spirit in you can help you to discern whether someone has really received the Lord. Like Peter, they should be able to say, "You are the Christ, the Son of the living God" (Matthew 16:16).

Jesus said in John 3:3, "I tell you the truth, no one can see the kingdom of God unless he is born again." He was emphasizing the need for the new birth before we can receive from God. So salvation comes first, and then we can ask for baptism with the Holy Spirit.

Paul asked some new disciples in Ephesus, "Did you receive the Holy Spirit when you believed?" They reported that they had "not even heard that there is a Holy Spirit" (Acts 19:2).

The Scriptures tell us, "On hearing this [Paul's teaching about Jesus], they were baptized into the name of the Lord Jesus. When Paul placed his hands on them, the Holy Spirit came on them, and they spoke in tongues and prophesied" (Acts 19:5–6). First there is perception—seeing the truth; then there is participation—entering into the truth. First there is faith in Jesus; then there naturally follows the overflowing of the Spirit. So you can lead people to Jesus, and then you can minister the baptism with the Spirit to them.

Bring Them Into the Presence of God
So what do you do when someone wants to receive the fullness of the Holy Spirit?

Be sure the seeker understands what they're asking for by questioning, "Have you come for the fullness of the Holy Spirit?" You can often tell from the look on the person's face, so don't interfere with their attitude of receiving by too many questions or words. You're simply there to join them in prayer.

Lead them to Jesus. Positively affirm that the presence of God is in the place and that He is welcoming all who come.

Sometimes the person ministering feels anxious about their role, and that tension does not help the person to receive. When I was seeking the baptism with the Holy Spirit, I had the feeling that if I didn't come through I would be a disappointment to the person praying. This just added to my sense that receiving the baptism was a very hard thing for which to strive.

Instead, get happy in the Holy Spirit and let it show. Let an atmosphere of faith begin to rise.

Take Promises from the Scriptures

Let the seeker know that they are going to receive the fullness of the Holy Spirit because the promise is for them.

Remind them of the promises in the Word of God. There is the original promise of Pentecost, spoken first by Peter: "You will receive the gift of the Holy Spirit. The promise is for you and your children and for all who are far off—for all whom the Lord our God will call" (Acts 2:38–39).

Remind them of the welcoming, comforting words of Jesus: "All that the Father gives me will come to me, and whoever comes to me I will never drive away" (John 6:37).

You can tell the person that Jesus urged us to persist in asking, confident in the goodness of the Giver:

> So I say to you: Ask and it will be given to you; seek and you will find; knock and the door will be opened to you. For everyone who asks receives; he who seeks finds; and to him who knocks, the door will be opened.
>
> Which of you fathers, if your son asks for a fish, will give him a snake instead? Or if he asks for an egg, will give him a scorpion? If you then, though you are evil, know how to give good gifts to your children, how much more will your Father in heaven give the Holy Spirit to those who ask him!
>
> Luke 11:9–13

Again, you can remind them that Jesus tells us to ask and to receive: "I tell you the truth, my Father will give you whatever you ask in my name. Until now you have not asked for anything in my name. Ask and you will receive, and your joy will be complete" (John 16:23–24).

We rest on the kindness and faithfulness of our Lord: "If God is for us, who can be against us? He who did not spare his own Son, but gave him up for us all—how will he not also, along with him, graciously give us all things?" (Romans 8:31–32).

Lay Hands on the Person

With the seeker's permission, lay your hands lightly on their head or shoulders. Lay hands on them to receive the Holy Spirit, as we have already read in Acts 19:6: "When Paul placed his hands on them, the Holy Spirit came on them." The grace of God is not resident in us to transmit, but God allows us to be channels.

Some people say, "I want it, I desire it, but I will be the only person in Christian history that cannot receive. It won't happen to me." That fear is not uncommon. Many struggle with unworthiness. Sometimes I feel as unspiritual as a toad—more likely to croak than to do anything else! Nevertheless, we can remind ourselves and others that the Lord Jesus has made us worthy vessels of His Holy Spirit.

Lead the person in prayer. Invite them to say,

> Holy Spirit, You are welcome to come in and fill me. I thank You, God, that You are pleased to dwell in the vessel of my life. You want to fill that vessel completely. Lord Jesus, I come to You. You received me though I had done nothing to earn it. You have made the vessel of my life clean and prepared to receive the fullness of the Holy Spirit.

Lead the person in praying, "Now, Lord Jesus, I ask You to fill me with the Holy Spirit. Lord, I believe Your Word that the promise is for me. Jesus, fill me now."

Encourage the Gift of Tongues

I never let a person go away without teaching them to expect the spiritual language. The gift of tongues is just part of the baptism with the Holy Spirit, enabling us to have eloquent communication with the heavenly Father.

Jesus promised the disciples, "These signs will accompany those who believe . . . they will speak in new tongues" (Mark 16:17). If Jesus endorsed it, it must be good. It is hard to believe that God would have started the church with something that was not important. The outpouring of the gift of tongues was vibrantly at the heart of what was going on at Pentecost.

Some people expect God to overwhelm them and seize their tongue to make it shape words, but it is usually as they worship and yield themselves as a child that the tongue comes. When children learn to speak, they go around babbling—they do not stay stone silent and suddenly come out with fully formed sentences!

That's why we encourage people to start praising God as they already know how to do. They can say to the Lord, "Even before I receive a new language of praise, I commit myself to a language of worship and praise. I will praise You with thanksgiving." Worship God with them, encouraging them to relax and allow the gift to flow out. One especially encouraging verse is from Hebrews 13:15: "Through Jesus, therefore, let us continually offer to God a sacrifice of praise—the fruit of lips that confess his name."

As people begin falteringly to use the gift, they frequently ask, "How do I know I'm not making it up?" Remind them that they have asked God in faith for His Holy Spirit. It is Jesus who promises to give the Holy Spirit, so would He let the devil push in? Encourage them, "You don't need to be afraid. Just go ahead and praise God." Eventually, the spiritual language of the Spirit will come as naturally as earthly speech. Let's be expectant before God that He can and will enable us as He promised.

Study questions:

1. Why is it important that other people receive the outpouring of the Holy Spirit?
2. What does it mean to be prophets and priests of God?
3. How do we bring people into the presence of the Lord as we pray for them?
4. What is the value of taking promises from Scripture and laying on hands?
5. Are you committed to sharing this precious gift of the baptism with the Spirit?

Jack Hayford is founding pastor of The Church on the Way in Van Nuys, California, and chancellor of The King's College and Seminary, an interdenominational ministry training center. He is the author of more than forty books and the host of a daily radio program and a weekly television program, both of which are broadcast around the world by Living Way Ministries.